The Story of Costume

All these figures appear in this book. See if you can find them!

The Story of Costume

John Peacock

with 328 color illustrations

Thames & Hudson

To Toby Peacock

© 2006 Thames & Hudson Ltd, London

All rights reserved. No part of this publication may be reproduced
or transmitted in any form or by any means, electronic or mechanical,
including photocopy, recording or any other information storage
and retrieval system, without prior permission in writing from
the publisher.

First published in 2006 in hardcover in the United States of America by
Thames & Hudson Inc., 500 Fifth Avenue, New York, New York 10110

thamesandhudsonusa.com

Library of Congress Catalog Card Number 2006900831

ISBN-13: 978-0-500-51309-5
ISBN-10: 0-500-51309-0

Printed and bound in China by C&C Offset

Contents

Introduction

Welcome to the wonderful world of historical costume. This is a world in which Egyptian queens wearing huge heavy wigs sit next to shaven-headed slaves in simple loincloths; where Robin Hood-era maidens wear beautiful flowing gowns and jewelled coronets; where seventeenth-century men wear fancy buckled shoes and big feathered hats; where little nineteenth-century boys look just like little nineteenth-century girls. This book presents hundreds of drawings of clothing worn by everyday people over four thousand years of fascinating history.

Our survey starts in Ancient Egypt, where we see the main fashions of this famous civilization. Next we visit Ancient Crete and Greece; then Ancient Babylon, Assyria and Persia; and then Ancient Rome and Byzantium. After that we look at the clothes worn after the time of the Romans. What follows next is a century-by-century survey of changing trends, right down to the present day.

Between the tenth and the sixteenth centuries (900–1600), costume evolved very slowly. After that, changes happened more and more quickly as trade flourished and people were able to buy cloth from all over the world. Techniques and machines were also invented that made clothing manufacture easier. By the end of the eighteenth century, upper-class ladies and gentlemen followed fashion very closely. Nowadays trends are followed by everybody.

The most incredible ideas have been adopted by fashionable people, for example the extremely pointed shoes worn by men in the fifteenth century, or the impractical bustle dresses worn by ladies in the nineteenth century, or the shorter-than-short mini skirts of the 1960s. Looking at these pictures might well make you wonder what people will be wearing in a hundred years' time, or what they will make of the clothes we wear today!

In the past fashions were created by wealthy people. Most of the examples illustrated are therefore those which, in general, were worn by the middle and upper-middle classes. On occasion, however, you will also see clothing worn by, for example, priests, soldiers, servants and workers. In addition, you will see from time to time clothing that was worn by children.

Along with the pictures there are notes that discuss each period illustrated. These notes point out the detail shown in the pictures and they also help you to see how a particular type or style of garment evolved over a period of time, becoming bigger or smaller, plainer or more elaborate, and so on.

When describing the clothes, well-known types of fabric have been mentioned, such as velvet, silk and satin. But there are many types of cloth that were worn in the past that are no longer familiar to us today. Have you, for example, heard of caffoy, harateen, lustering or moreen? These fabrics are not mentioned in these pages but they were all very common in their day.

At the end of the book there are two pages that chart the development of costume from Antiquity to the present day. Looking at the chart you can see at a glance the main changes that have taken place over the centuries.

Finally, at the very back of the book is a bibliography listing publications that I found useful when preparing this volume. If you would like to know more about the subject of costume and fashion, I hope you will find this list of interest, too.

John Peacock

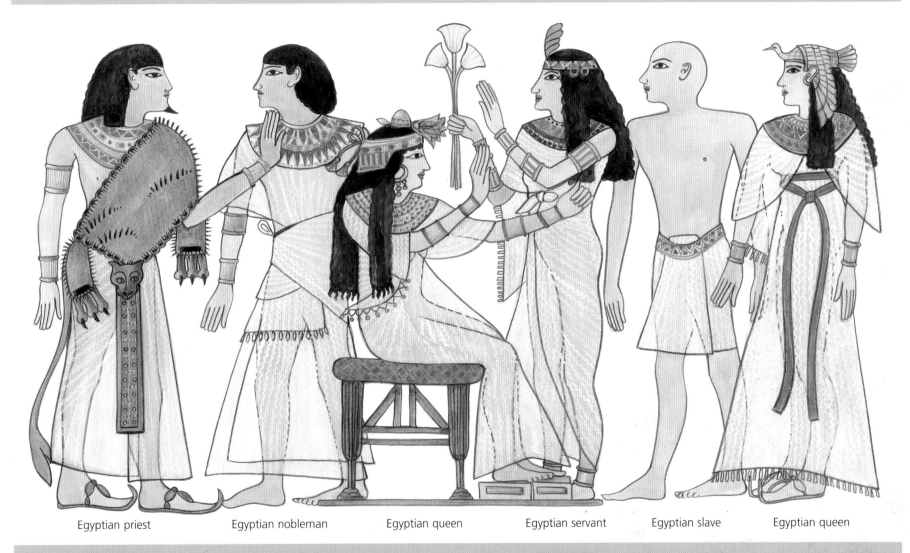

Egyptian priest Egyptian nobleman Egyptian queen Egyptian servant Egyptian slave Egyptian queen

The Ancient Egyptians wore few clothes. Many high-ranking men liked to wear short aprons of fine pleated linen, known as **loincloths,** and ankle-length **shirts** with wide sleeves. Well-to-do women wrapped ankle-length **gowns** of see-through pleated linen around their bodies and tied them high at the waist. Both men and women wore **jewelry** – wide collars, bangles and anklets. Both also shaved their heads and wore curled **wigs**. Popular footwear included **sandals** with up-turned toes. Poor people dressed more simply: slaves often went naked.

Cretan man and woman   Greek woman   Greek hunter   Greek girl   Greek nobleman

Men in Ancient Crete wore little apart from a short, close-fitting **shirt** or a loincloth. Women in Ancient Crete wore a **dress** with a long, bell-shaped skirt and fitted top. People in Ancient Greece did not usually sew their clothes together, but wrapped them around their bodies. Men mainly wore shirts called **chitons**, which were pinned on each shoulder and worn with a belt. Women's chitons were similar, though usually long. Sometimes **patterns** were painted down the sides or around the neck. People did not wear much jewelry, but sandals and **short boots** were common.

Babylonian guard   Assyrian hunter   Persian king   Assyrian king   Assyrian queen

Fashions in Ancient Babylon, Assyria and Persia were quite similar, and remained so for a long time. Both men and women wore T-shaped, ankle-length **tunics** in brightly dyed cloths, often painted all over with patterns. **Capes** and **shawls** with heavy fringes were also popular. People usually went barefoot, or else they wore **sandals** or soft leather **ankle boots**. Both men and women wore **bangles** and **earrings**. They also liked flat-topped **hats**, wide **headbands** and tall **crowns**. Men and women had long curled hair, and men had beards and moustaches.

Roman noblewoman   Roman boy   Roman nobleman   Roman soldier   Byzantine man and woman

The clothes worn by the people of Ancient Rome were similar to those of the Ancient Greeks. Men wore long shawls of fine wool, known as **togas**, draped in various ways over a long or a short T-shaped **tunic**. Women wore draped cloth over a tunic known as a **stola**. Sometimes women also wore a long **veil** attached to a headdress. Roman soldiers wore metal **chest-plates**. People wore soft leather **boots** outside, and indoors they wore sandals. In Ancient Byzantium rich people wore brightly dyed clothes as well as **gold jewelry** set with precious stones.

English farm worker   French peasant woman   English man   French soldier   German lady and gentleman

Early European costume was simple and practical. People wore T-shaped **tunics** that were either short or long. They wore one tunic on top of another. They also wore **cloaks** and **shawls**. Most garments were made from woven wool or linen. During this time the rich and the poor wore clothes of the same type. What made them different was the quality of the material and the cost of the trimmings and decorations, such as embroidery, fur lining, jewelled belts and brooches. Everyone wore long or short **boots**, or they tied **strips** of cloth or leather around their legs.

German man   German woman   English lady   English nobleman   French man   English lady

Throughout this century styles stayed much as before. Men continued to wear knee- or ankle-length woollen **tunics** over a long-sleeved **undershirt**. They also wore small **hats**, often decorated with a **brooch**. Well-dressed ladies liked to cover their hair with a **veil**, and they wore long, close-fitting **gowns**, often in light blue, pink or green. Sometimes the gowns had embroidered or woven **borders** at the neck and the hem. Dainty **hip belts** were also popular. Everyone wore soft leather **shoes**. Men wore long **stockings**, which they strapped with leather thongs.

English man   English farmer   Flemish nobleman   French queen   English lady   German nobleman

During the twelfth century, with a few exceptions, clothes were made in similar ways and styles to previous centuries. Men wore short, belted **tunics**, though some preferred a mid-calf-length tunic that had wide sleeves and was worn over an ankle-length **undershirt**. Small **hats**, sometimes trimmed with fur, were also popular. Ladies' **dresses** often had sleeves with **cuffs** that trailed right down to the ground. Ladies grew their hair very long and **braided** it with false hair and bright ribbons. They also liked to wear jewelled **coronets** that held short veils in place.

Italian noblewoman   German lady   English noblewoman   German man   English nobleman   English pilgrim

The thirteenth century brought richly patterned and brightly dyed materials. Wealthy men wore long woollen **tunics**, often split at the front and decorated with embroidered designs. For ladies, long **overdresses** with deep armholes became popular. **Hats** and **headgear** of all shapes and sizes were worn. One new fashion for women was to wrap a **band of linen** under the chin and all the way around the head. Both men and women wore floor-length **cloaks** that fastened across the chest with a cord between two brooches or a single clasp at the front.

Flemish woman   German boy   German gentleman   English knight   English man   Spanish priest   English lady

Rare and costly fabrics were used during this period, though with little pattern or decoration. Men sometimes wore an ankle-length **coat** that had deep armholes but no sleeves. The coat was open at the front and had a short **cape** and **hood**. Fashionable men also wore a close-fitting linen **cap** with a strap under the chin. Knights wore **chain-mail** to protect them. Ladies' **dresses** were often loose-fitting, falling in folds from a high waist. Everyone used small money purses that hung from **belts**. Leather **shoes** were also worn, often with a strap over the front.

English lady   English gentleman   English farm worker   French country woman   French lady   English lady   English man

Though both rich and poor men wore **shoulder capes** with long pointed hoods, there was generally a huge difference between the clothing of the nobility and that of the working classes. Poor people wore clothes that were simple, practical and **plain**. Rich men sometimes wore clothing that had **one side** different to the other. Ladies liked to wear **gowns** that had low necklines and tight sleeves, with long trailing **cuffs** from elbow-level. Men wore **piked poulaines**, which were shoes with long pointed toes. Women's shoes were less pointed.

English prince   French lady   German lady   English lady   German man   English man

Well-to-do men and women wore tight-fitting clothes in rich velvets and silks. Some men wore a short **tunic** with a high collar and buttons down the front. Other tunics were ankle-length, with fur trimming and lining. Men's **hats** were like padded cushions, with fabric draped on top. Ladies wore **dresses** with a high waist, a trailing skirt and trailing sleeves. The edges of the **sleeves** were often cut into fancy patterns such as leaves or petals. Men's leather shoes, ankle boots and stockings had very long **pointed toes**. Women's shoes were less pointed.

French nobleman   English gentleman   German gentleman   English woman   German lady   Italian lady

France and Italy produced richly patterned silks and velvets, which were sold everywhere. Some men wore a long **coat** with embroidered trailing sleeves. Others wore a short **tunic** with baggy sleeves. Men's **stockings** often had leather soles. It was fashionable for rich people to wear a string of **bells** attached to their clothes. Ladies often wore a plain **underdress** with tight sleeves. On top they would wear a flower-patterned, high-waisted **gown** with wide flowing sleeves and a long skirt. Women's hair was usually hidden under a **headdress** and stiffened see-through **veil**.

English lady   Italian princess   English man   Italian man   Flemish servant   English jester

During this period fabrics printed with large patterns were very popular with both men and women. Young men often wore a short tight **tunic**, which had long tight sleeves and short puffed over-sleeves, together with a mid-calf-length sleeveless **coat**. Men's **hats** were generally quite small. Women sometimes wore a long open **coat** which fastened across the front with straps of gold braid. The coat had large sleeves decorated with **pearls** and **ribbons**. Young women wore their hair down, with small but elaborate **headdresses** decorated with pearls.

Flemish man   German lady   French noblewoman   English lady   French man   Italian man

In this period men's **tunics** were either short or long. Some had wide shoulders, large puffed sleeves and high collars. Others had pleated skirts and fur trimming. Men's **hats** were generally small, and sometimes they were carried over the shoulder on a wide **ribbon**. Fashionable women wore **dresses** with a tight-fitting top, a low neckline and see-through sleeves. Everyone found **belts** useful for carrying things such as money purses, perfume bottles or keys. Women and men also started to wear more **jewelry** in the form of brooches, necklaces, belts and buttons.

French lady and gentleman   German lord   Dutch noblewoman   English gentleman   English princess

Men wore long **coats** made from thick cloth, with fur collars and lining. The sleeves were baggy and had a large hole to show off the sleeve of the **tunic** underneath. Men's **hats** were usually small, and sometimes they had a **brooch** to decorate the turned-back brim. Ladies liked **gowns** that had tight tops, low square necklines and large puffed sleeves with decorative slashes cut in them. Some ladies wore large **hats** decorated with feathers (men wore these, too). Other ladies wore small black **caps** with pleats at the front and a long veil at the back to hide their hair.

German gentleman   German lady   English noblewoman   Spanish gentleman   Spanish lady   English gentleman

Men made their shoulders look broader by adding a **wide collar** above the huge puffed sleeves of their knee-length coats. Pleated cotton collars and cuffs showed from above the neck and below the sleeves of their **undertunics**. Matching fancy shorts, known as **breeches**, were also popular, as were flat **caps** with feathers. Ladies' **gowns** had stiffened tops with low square necklines and tight sleeves with wide fur cuffs. The bell-shaped **skirts** were open at the front to show off embroidered **petticoats** underneath. Some **hats** looked like the pointed roof of a house.

English lady   French princess   Spanish gentleman   English girl   Italian man   Spanish gentleman

Well-to-do ladies and gentlemen often wore clothes that were covered with tiny **slashes** to show the rich linings underneath. Fine embroidery was also very popular. Fashionable men, with moustaches and pointed beards, wore fancy padded **breeches**, knitted stockings known as **hose**, and short jackets known as **doublets**. Ladies liked to wear **belts** with long hanging ends, often set with precious jewels. People began to wear pleated **ruffs** around the neck and wrists. **Shoes** had narrower toes than before. Children were dressed in the same styles as their parents.

English falconer   Spanish lady   English queen   French gentleman   Italian lady

Rich, bright fabrics, combined with fine embroidery, precious jewels and pearls, made the fashions at court lavish and extravagant. Gentlemen wore short padded **breeches** and tight-fitting **doublets** covered in gold braid. Tiny **slashes** in clothing were still popular. Rich people's **ruffs** became so big that sometimes they had to be supported with wires. Grand ladies decorated their tight **bodices** and full **skirts** with jewelled brooches and ropes of pearls. Folding **fans** were first seen at this time, too. **Shoes** were delicate and often made from silk or velvet.

Dutch servant   English man   English lady   English lady   French gentleman   Spanish girl

Wide, turned-down **collars** gradually replaced the stiff ruffs of the previous period. Swords and daggers were worn suspended from leather **belts**, and **hats** had wide brims. Thigh-length leather **boots** with low heels were popular for men. Ladies wore a high **collar** of fine lace to frame the face. Their **gowns** had a stiff bodice with a low neckline. The wide skirt, known as a **farthingale**, was supported over a frame and split at the front to display the embroidered **petticoat** underneath. Ladies also wore corsets, or **stays**, to make their waists fashionably small.

English man   French lady   English lady   Dutch girl   English country woman   English gentleman

This was the age of **lace**. Men's high-waisted **jackets** had lace collars and cuffs. Ladies' **gowns** had low necklines with large lace-edged collars. Matching lace cuffs were turned back over big puffed sleeves. Well-dressed men wore **silk ribbons** tied under their knees to hold up their knitted stockings. Matching **bows** decorated the fronts of high-heeled shoes. People attached iron frames, known as **pattens**, to their shoes to keep them out of the mud. Long **gauntlet gloves** were fashionable, and ladies liked to wear earrings, necklaces and bracelets made of **pearls**.

English man   English Puritan woman and man   French nobleman   French lady   French gentleman

Some religious people thought it was wicked to wear rich and costly clothes, so they dressed in **plain** garments with white collars and cuffs, and they cut their **hair** short. Meanwhile rich people continued to wear their expensive fashions in velvets, silks and satins. Men's coats were decorated with **ribbons** and **bows**, and so were the low, off-the-shoulder gowns of well-to-do ladies. Gentlemen wore long curled **wigs** and they sported thin moustaches. It was fashionable to wear **shoes** with red high heels, as well as **'bucket top' boots** with metal spurs at the heel.

English lady   Dutch woman   Italian gentleman   French gentleman   English gentleman   English lady

Fashions changed only slightly in this period. Gentlemen's **wigs** became larger and fell in heavy curls onto the shoulders. **Coats** had wide, stiffened skirts and were worn open to show the long **waistcoat** (or "vest") underneath. **Shoes** with high tongues, silver buckles and high heels were fashionable. Ladies' **gowns** had a stiffened bodice and a long skirt that was split at the front and gathered up at the back to reveal the **petticoat**. Some ladies wore a tall **headdress** of looped ribbons and lace. Fashionable people also carried a **fur muff** to keep their hands warm.

Italian man   English lady   English lady   French man   English lady   English woman

Gentlemen of this time liked to wear a **scarf** tied around the neck. They also wore a **coat** that was stiffened to make its skirts stand out. The wide **cuffs** of the coat were turned back to show the white **shirt** underneath. Leather **shoes** with silver buckles were popular, and it was fashionable to carry a **walking stick**. Ladies wore **gowns** with low-cut necklines trimmed with lace. Materials were often embroidered with stripes of pretty flowers. Sometimes the gown fell loosely from the shoulders at the back. Small frilled **caps** with ribbon streamers were popular.

English lady   French court lady   English man   French court gentleman   English lady

Men's **wigs**, sometimes covered with powder, became smaller at this time and fitted closely to their wearer's head. They had **curls** on either side and a pigtail tied into a bow at the back. Three-cornered hats were also very popular. Ladies wore wide **skirts** that were supported with whalebone hoops underneath. The skirts were sometimes open at the front to show quilted **petticoats**. Silks and satins embroidered with flowers were fashionable. Ladies wore **straw hats** with ribbons that tied under the chin, and they often carried a pretty **parasol** on a long handle.

English soldier   English gentleman   French lady   French lady   American lady   French man

Towards the end of this period gentlemen wore plain **coats** with stand-up collars. The coats were left open to show off tight **waistcoats** and **knee breeches** underneath. Men's **shoes** had large silver buckles. Fashionable ladies wore **gowns** with three-quarter-length sleeves. The gowns were made from brocades and silks – often in pale green, golden yellow or pale blue – with embroidered or painted patterns. Fine cotton **scarves** were tied around their low necklines. Ladies also wore elaborate **wigs** powdered with flour and decorated with feathers.

French man   English lady   French lady   French revolutionary   French lady   English gentleman

Towards the end of this period powdered wigs had disappeared. Men's **hair** was cut short and ladies wore theirs in **ringlets** at the back. Men's **jackets** were short at the front and cut away into tails at the back. **Breeches** were close-fitting and buttoned at the knee. Male revolutionaries in France wore ankle-length **trousers**. Ladies liked to wear high-waisted **gowns** and a frilled scarf, known as a **fichu**, tied around their low neckline. Ladies often wore **riding costumes** with a fitted jacket and full skirt, and a big hat like those worn by men.

French lady   American gentleman   French lady   English gentleman   English boy   English man

At the beginning of this new century there were many changes in costume. Long **pantaloons** became the fashion for men, complete with straps, or **stirrups**, under heelless shoes. **Shirts** with stand-up pointed collars were worn with **neck scarves**. Men of all classes wore **top hats**. At the beginning of the period high-waisted cotton **dresses** were fashionable for ladies. They were worn with fine wool **shawls**. Later dresses became shorter to show off silk **shoes**. Long **gloves** and folding **fans** were popular for eveningwear. Little boys were dressed like little girls.

English lady   English boy   American schoolmistress   English man   German man   French girl   English lady

Men wore long **trousers** and their **coats** were now longer and fuller, with velvet collars. Fancy **waistcoats** were also popular. Silk scarves, known as **cravats**, were tied around the neck under stiff shirt collars. Tall **'stove pipe' hats** were also common. Ladies had tiny corseted waists and very full skirts worn over a lot of stiffened petticoats. They wore pretty **bonnets** with ribbon ties under the chin. Fashionable **parasols** were carried, as well as short **gloves** and tiny **bags**. Little girls wore similar fashions to ladies but with shorter skirts and long, lace-edged knickers.

English lady   French lady   French lady   German man   French boy   English postman

Men and women now wore different clothes in the evening. Gentlemen always wore **gloves**, and they had black wool **suits** with tight jackets and trousers. They also wore white waistcoats, shirts and neck cloths. Necklines on ladies' **evening dresses** were wide and low-cut, leaving the shoulders bare. Skirts became so full that they had to be supported over hooped whalebone or wire petticoats, known as **crinolines**. Ladies used **fans** and wore short **gloves**. When riding, they put on a **top hat** like those worn by men. People like postmen wore special **uniforms**.

German lady and gentleman   French lady   French girl   French lady   French girl   English gentleman

Short **overcoats** with velvet collars and cuffs were popular for men, as were **bowler hats** and narrow **bow-ties** and **neck-ties**. Men also liked to have moustaches and long sideburns. For women, the very wide **skirts** of the previous period became smaller, with the fullness gathered towards the back and supported over horsehair pads or wire frames to make an oval shape. The arrival of the sewing machine made it possible to attach large quantities of pleated and fringed **trimming** to clothing. **Hats** were small and had pretty ribbons that tied under the chin.

English lady   German man   American man   French lady   English lady   German man

Although men still wore **bowler hats** or **top hats**, their clothes became more like those worn in modern times. **Overcoats** with fur collars and cuffs were popular. Still fashionable for ladies at the beginning of this period was the **bustle pad**, worn below the waist at the back of the skirt to make it stand out. **Hats** with fur trimming were also worn. At the end of the period women's **dresses** had high necks, huge leg o' mutton sleeves and flared skirts. Wide-brimmed, feather-trimmed **hats** were very fashionable, and long **umbrellas** were often carried.

English lady   English man   German girl   French lady   German lady   American man

Fashionable summer clothes for men included striped cotton **jackets** with patch pockets, flannel **trousers** with sharp creases and turn-up cuffs, and **shirts** worn with stiff turned-down collars and bow-ties. Straw **boater hats** were worn in summer. **Felt hats** with soft brims were popular in winter. The floor-length flowing skirts and fine lace trimmings worn by ladies at the beginning of the century gave way to mid-calf-length **skirts** with fur-trimmed hems, revealing long, buttoned **boots** with high heels. Large, fur-trimmed **hats** and **fur muffs** were popular accessories.

English man   American man   English man   English lady   English girl   English lady   French lady   English lady

Men's clothes were generally plain and remained much as before. Belted **raincoats** were popular, as were double-breasted **jackets** and **coats**, their two rows of buttons on display. **Walking sticks** were the usual accessory. In the 1920s ladies wore short dresses, silk stockings, shoes with pointed toes and **brimless hats** pulled down above their eyes. Long **bead necklaces** were fashionable and hair was cut short. In the 1930s **evening dresses** were made from satin and clung to the body. **Shoes** were dyed to match the dress. **Hair** was permanently waved ("permed").

English woman and man

English woman

French woman

English man   American man

Sports jackets, worn with flannel trousers, were popular for men throughout this period. Casual lace-up **shoes** and soft felt **hats** were fashionable, too. Hair was cut short. The early 1940s women wore **jackets** with wide padded shoulders and knee-length pleated **skirts**. Small hats, handleless clutch bags, gauntlet gloves and sling-back, peep-toe shoes were all popular accessories. By the end of the period, **dresses** had tightly fitted bodices and full, mid-calf-length skirts. Hair was curled and cut short. Men's and women's **sportswear** was similar to their everyday wear.

French woman   English girl   English man   English man   American woman   English man   French woman

Fashionable men in the 1950s wore leather **tops** with knitted sleeves, tight-fitting **trousers** and **shoes** with pointed toes. Hooded **duffel coats** were also popular at the beginning of this period. **Suede jackets** were the fashion in the 1960s. Women of the 1950s wore **dresses** with tight-fitting bodices, wide belts, knee-length skirts supported over stiffened petticoats, and **shoes** with pointed toes and high stiletto heels. By the end of the period women were wearing mini skirts and **mini dresses**, together with **tights** and knee-high, flat-heeled **boots**.

German man   French woman   Italian man   English woman   Italian woman   American woman

Men and women wore **flared trousers** ("bellbottoms"). Men grew their hair and had long sideburns. Short **leather jackets** with zip fastenings were popular, and sometimes collars were worn turned up at the back. High-necked **polo sweaters** were also popular. Many women wore **trouser suits** and workman-type **overalls**, often with embroidered hems. In the 1970s **platform shoes** were also popular with men and women. In the early 1980s **padded shoulders** and **big sleeves** were fashionable for day and evening. **Hair** was very curly and women liked big **earrings**.

American man   Italian woman   French woman   Italian man   English man   English woman

In the mid-1980s **trousers** were narrow and Italian **knitwear** with padded shoulders was popular for both men and women. On formal occasions men liked to wear a long **jacket**, a bright **waistcoat** and a patterned **neck-tie**. Women's **skirts** were very short and the shoulders of their **jackets** very wide. Long-handled leather **shoulder bags** were also popular, as were big hats and artificial flowers. To start with, it was fashionable for women to have long curly hair. Later many men and women had their hair cut short and sometimes they had dyed streaks added.

Ancient Egypt

Ancient Crete

Ancient Greece

Ancient Persia and Assyria

Ancient Rome

Byzantium

After the Romans

1000

1100

1200

1250

1300

1350

1400

1430

1465

1500

1525

1550

1575

1600   1625   1650   1675   1700   1725

1750   1775   1800   1820   1840   1860   1880

1900   1920   1935   1950   1970   1985   present day

The following are some of the publications that were very useful in the preparation of this book:

Anderson Black, J., and Madge Garland, *A History of Fashion*, London, 1975
Boucher, François, *A History of Costume in the West*, London, 1965
Bradfield, Nancy, *Costume in Detail: Women's Dress 1730–1930*, London, 1968
Bruhn, Wolfgang, and Max Tilke, *A Pictorial History of Costume*, London, 1955
Carnegy, Vicky, *Fashions of a Decade: The 1980s*, London, 1990
Carter, Ernestine, *The Changing World of Fashion: 1900 to the Present Day*, London, 1977
Contini, Mila, *Fashion: From Ancient Egypt to the Present Day*, London, 1965
Cunnington, C. Willett, and Phillis Cunnington, *Handbook of Mediaeval Costume*, London, 1952
Cunnington, Phillis, *Costume of Household Servants from the Middle Ages to 1900*, London, 1974
De Marley, Diana, *Fashion for Men: An Illustrated History*, London, 1985
Dorner, Jane, *Fashion in the Twenties and Thirties*, London, 1973
___, *Fashion in the Forties and Fifties*, London, 1975
Drake, Nicholas, *The Fifties in Vogue*, New York, 1987
Ewing, Elizabeth, *History of Twentieth Century Fashion*, London, 1974
___, *History of Children's Costume*, London, 1977
___, *Fur in Dress*, London, 1981
Gorsline, Douglas, *What People Wore: A Visual History of Dress from Ancient Times to the Twentieth Century*, London, 1978
Halls, Zillah, *Men's Costume 1580–1750*, Her Majesty's Stationary Office, London, 1970
___, *Women's Costume 1600–1750*, Her Majesty's Stationary Office, London, 1970
___, *Women's Costume 1750–1800*, Her Majesty's Stationary Office, London, 1972
Hamilton Hill, Margot, and Peter Bucknell, *The Evolution of Fashion: Pattern and Cut from 1066 to 1930*, London, 1967
Hansen, Henny Harald, *Costume Cavalcade*, London, 1956
Hartley, Dorothy, *Mediaeval Costume and Life*, London, 1931

Houston, Mary G., *Ancient Greek, Roman and Byzantine Costume and Decorations*, London, 1930
___, *European Costume from the Thirteenth Century to the Commencement of the Seventeenth Century with Decorations*, London, 1930
___, *Mediaeval Costume in England and France: the 13th, 14th and 15th Centuries*, London, 1939
Houston, Mary G., and Florence S. Hornblower, *Ancient Egyptian, Assyrian and Persian Costume and Decorations*, London, 1920
Kohler, Carl, *A History of Costume*, London, 1928
Laver, James, *Costume Through the Ages*, London, 1963
___, *Costume in Antiquity*, London, 1964
___, *A Concise History of Costume*, London, 1969
McDowell, Colin, *Forties Fashion and the New Look*, London, 1997
Mulvagh, Jane, *Vogue: History of Twentieth Century Fashion*, London, 1988
O'Hara, Georgina, *The Encyclopaedia of Fashion from 1840 to the 1980s*, London, 1986
Racinet, Albert, *The Encyclopaedia of Costume*, London, 1988
Robinson, Julian, *Fashion in the Forties*, London, 1976
___, *Fashion in the Thirties*, London, 1978
Scott, Margaret, *Late Gothic Europe: 1400–1500*, London, 1980
Unstead, R. J., *Looking at History: From Cavemen to the Present Day*, London, 1963
Volcino, Michele, *Storia del Costume*, Rome, 1961
Waugh, Nora, *Corsets and Crinolines*, London, 1954
___, *The Cut of Men's Clothes: 1600–1900*, London, 1964
___, *The Cut of Women's Clothes: 1600–1930*, London, 1973
Wilcox, R. Turner, *The Mode in Costume*, New York, 1948
___, *Five Centuries of American Costume*, New York, 1963
___, *The Dictionary of Costume*, New York, 1970.